A Day in the Life: Rain Forest Animals

Orangutan

Anita Ganeri

Heinemann Library
Chicago, IL

www.heinemannraintree.com
Visit our website to find out more information about Heinemann-Raintree books.

To order:

☎ Phone 888-454-2279

▣ Visit www.heinemannraintree.com to browse our catalog and order online.

Edited by Nancy Dickmann, Rebecca Rissman, and Catherine Veitch
Designed by Steve Mead
Picture research by Mica Brancic
Originated by Capstone Global Library
Printed and bound in China by South China Printing Company Ltd

14 13 12 11 10
10 9 8 7 6 5 4 3 2 1

Library of Congress Cataloging-in-Publication Data
Ganeri, Anita, 1961-
   Orangutan / Anita Ganeri.
      p. cm.—(A day in the life. Rain forest animals)
   Includes bibliographical references and index.
   ISBN 978-1-4329-4107-9 (hc)—ISBN 978-1-4329-4118-5 (pb) 1. Orangutan—Juvenile literature. I. Title.
   QL737.P96G366 2011
   599.88'3—dc22

9673   2010000966

Acknowledgments
We would like to thank the following for permission to reproduce photographs: Alamy p. 10 (© Jeroen Hendriks); Ardea pp. 11, 22 (Thomas Marent); Corbis pp. 4, 23 mammal (© Theo Allofs), 6 (© Tom Brakefield), 7, 23 pouch (© DLILLC), 17 (© W. Perry Conway), 19 (© Warren Jacobi), 21 (epa/© FRISO GENTSCH); FLPA pp. 5, 23 ape (Jurgen & Christine Sohns), 12, 23 rubbery (Minden Pictures/Jeffrey Oonk/FN), 13 (Minden Pictures/Cyril Ruoso), 15, 18 (Minden Pictures/Thomas Marent); Nature Picture Library pp. 14, 20, 23 vine (© Anup Shah); Photolibrary pp. 9 (David Maitland), 16 (imagebroker.net/ROM ROM); Shutterstock p. 23 rain forest (© Szefei).

Cover photograph of an adult orangutan with an infant reproduced with permission of Corbis (© Frans Lanting).

Back cover photographs of (left) a male orangutan reproduced with permission of Corbis (© DLILLC); and (right) an orangutan's nest reproduced with permission of Nature Picture Library (© Anup Shah).

We would like to thank Michael Bright for his invaluable help in the preparation of this book.

Every effort has been made to contact copyright holders of material reproduced in this book. Any omissions will be rectified in subsequent printings if notice is given to the publisher.

Contents

Some words are in bold, **like this**. You can find them in the glossary on page 23.

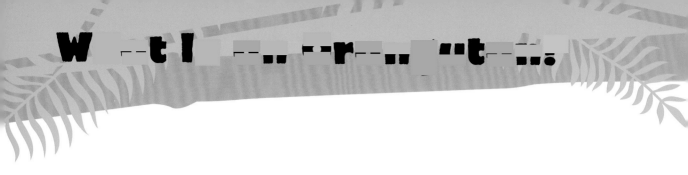

An orangutan is a **mammal**.

Many mammals have hairy bodies and feed their babies milk.

chimpanzee

Orangutans belong to a group of mammals known as **apes**.

Chimpanzees and gorillas are also types of apes.

What Does an Orangutan Look Like?

Orangutans have large bodies that are covered in long, red-brown hair.

They have very long, strong arms.

6

cheek

pouch

Male orangutans are bigger than females.

An adult male has big cheeks and a baggy **pouch** around its neck.

Where Do Orangutans Live?

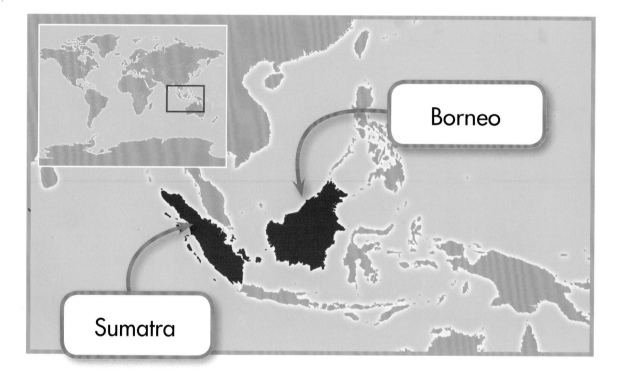

Orangutans live on the islands of Borneo and Sumatra in Southeast Asia.

They live in the **rain forests** that grow on the islands.

Orangutans spend most of their time high up in the rain forest trees.

They do not come down to the ground very often.

What Does It Do During the Day?

An orangutan wakes up when the sun rises.

It has a snack of fruit for breakfast.

After breakfast, an orangutan has a short rest before it starts the day.

Then it spends most of the day looking for food among the trees.

What Do Orangutans Eat and Drink?

Orangutans mainly eat fruit, leaves, and other parts of plants.

An orangutan picks a piece of fruit, then peels it with its teeth and **rubbery** lips.

It rains every day in the **rain forest**.

When an orangutan feels thirsty, it scoops up rainwater from a hole in a tree to drink.

How Do Orangutans Move Around?

vine

An orangutan rocks on a branch or **vine**.

It does this until it is close enough to grab another branch or vine.

hand

The orangutan always holds onto a tree with at least one hand and one foot.

Its hands and feet are shaped like hooks for grabbing hold of branches.

Male orangutans usually live on their own.

They do not help look after young orangutans.

A young orangutan lives with its mother until it is about eight years old.

Its mother teaches it where to find food in the **rain forest**.

A male orangutan can be very noisy.

He can puff up his neck **pouch** and make a loud roaring sound.

This sound can be heard from far away in the **rain forest**.

It warns other orangutans to stay away from the tree where the male is feeding.

nest

In the evening, an orangutan uses leaves and twigs to build a nest.

The nest is where the orangutan sleeps.

Baby orangutans are born in the nest at night.

When they are older, their mother shows them how to make nests.

hand

fur

arm

eye

ear

cheek

throat pouch

ape large, human-like mammal, such as orangutans and chimpanzees

mammal animal that feeds its babies milk. Most mammals have hair or fur.

pouch baggy piece of skin

rain forest thick forest with very tall trees and a lot of rain

rubbery soft and bendable

vine long, dangling plant that grows in the rain forest

Fi.. ---t M--r

Books

Bredeson, Carmen. *Orangutans Up Close.* Berkeley Heights, NJ
   Enslow Elementary, 2009.

Mattern, Joanne. *Orangutans.* Mankato, MN: Capstone Press,
   2010.

Websites

http://kids.nationalgeographic.com/Animals/CreatureFeature/
   Orangutan

www.a-z-animals.com/animals/orang-utan/

www.sandiegozoo.org/animalbytes/t-orangutan.html

Index